To _____

From _____

Other giftbooks in the same series by Exley:
Missing You...   Bon Voyage   Daughters...
Sisters...   When Love is Forever Mothers...
True Love...   For a Good Friend   Brothers!

Published simultaneously in 1996 by Exley Publications in Great Britain, and
Exley Publications LLC in the USA.

12 11 10 9

Border illustrations by Juliette Clarke
Edited and pictures selected by Helen Exley

ISBN 1-85015-792-8

Picture research by Image Select International.
Typeset by Delta, Watford.
Printed in China.

Exley Publications Ltd, 16 Chalk Hill, Watford, Herts. WD19 4BG, UK.
Exley Publications LLC, 232 Madison Avenue, Suite 1409, NY 10016, USA.
www.helenexleygiftbooks.com

SONS...

QUOTATIONS SELECTED BY
*H*ELEN EXLEY

EXLEY
NEW YORK • WATFORD, UK

The door bursts open.
"Look what I've found!"
"Guess what I've seen?"
"Come *quick* or you'll miss
the rainbow,
... the woodpecker,
... the pony and trap,
... the Jenson Interceptor,
... the flock of swans!!!"
Thank you for putting exclamation
marks in my life.

PAM BROWN, b.1928

A child enters your home and makes so much noise for twenty years you can hardly stand it – then departs, leaving the house so silent you think you will go mad.

DR. J.A. HOLMES

A son can be guaranteed to astound you all through his life – astound, bewilder, unnerve, flabbergast....
You name it. He'll do it.

CHARLOTTE GRAY

A small son can charm himself into, and out of, most things.
– Some never give up trying.

JENNY DE VRIES

Boys are found everywhere –
on top of, underneath, inside
of, climbing on, swinging
from, running around or
jumping to. Mothers love
them, little girls hate them,
older sisters and brothers
tolerate them, adults ignore
them and Heaven protects
them. A boy is Truth with dirt
on its face, Beauty with a cut
on its finger, Wisdom with
bubble gum in its hair and the
Hope of the future with a frog
in its pocket.

ALAN BECK,
FROM "WHAT IS A BOY?"

Every baby born into the world is a finer one than the last.

CHARLES DICKENS (1812-1870)

I saw pure love when my son looked at me, and I knew that I had to make a good life for the two of us....

SUZANNE SOMERS, b.1950

*H*ow could I have forgotten the hush that waits the gathering storm, willow luminous in the uncanny light, white birds wheeling across the massing cloud? The first fat drops on the bone dry ground, the drumming on the roof, the rattle against the window panes, the gush of overflowing gutters, the regiments of raindrops marching along the street.

The fading from ferocity to gentleness. The glow

of traffic signals on roads. The pattering of droplets from the trees. Birdsong. The smell of grass and leaves and earth after the storm has passed.

I had forgotten them, Son – reduced them to "Looks like rain" and "Good thing we made it home." Until you took my hand and, through your wondering eyes, I rediscovered them.

PAM BROWN, b.1928

A baby's love for his mother is probably the sweetest emotion we can savor. When my son heard my voice at the downstairs door he'd begin to sing, and when I arrived in his view he'd fall back on his fat legs, his behind would thud to the floor and he'd laugh, his big head rocking up and down.

MAYA ANGELOU, b.1928,
FROM "GATHER TOGETHER IN MY NAME"

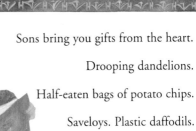

Sons bring you gifts from the heart.

Drooping dandelions.

Half-eaten bags of potato chips.

Saveloys. Plastic daffodils.

Pop-eyed plaster pug dogs.

Cans of lager.

Strange scent.

Secondhand books – tatty or antique.

Hugs.

PAM BROWN, b.1928

Once Knute playfully demanded of one of the
boys an account of his age. He answered, "Seven."
"Impossible," his father said; "no young man
could possibly get quite so dirty in seven years."
Then he tried to placate the boy's mother with a
grotesquely penitential look.

BONNIE ROCKNE, FROM A NOTE IN HER
HUSBAND'S AUTOBIOGRAPHY

Sons eat odd socks, shoes, best shirts,
underpants elastic and combs.
There is no other explanation.

ROSANNE AMBROSE-BROWN

WHAT IS A BOY?

What are little boys made of?
Frogs and snails
And puppy-dogs' tails,
That's what little boys are made of.

NURSERY RHYMES (1844)
(J.O. HALLIWELL)

Boys are capital fellows in their own way,
among their mates; but they are
unwholesome companions for grown people.

CHARLES LAMB (1775-1834),
FROM "*ESSAYS OF ELIA*"

A boy is a magical creature – you can lock him out of your workshop, but you can't lock him out of your heart. You can get him out of your study, but you can't get him out of your mind. Might as well give up – he is your captor, your jailer, your boss and your master – a freckled-faced, pint-sized, cat-chasing bundle of noise.

ALAN BECK,
FROM *"WHAT IS A BOY?"*

From the very instant that I saw your big/little feet poking out from the basket in my room in the hospital on January 16, 1971, I have valued and respected and loved you unconditionally. With all of the fabulous adventures I have had in this first half of my life, it has been our friendship and trust that have been the biggest gift.

ALI MACGRAW, IN A LETTER
TO HER SON JOSHUA,
FROM *"MOVING PICTURES"*

Sons value a swan's feather, a silver hub-cap, a
speckled stone. They gather together empty cans
small bottles, marbles swirled and striped,
skeleton leaves, keys to forgotten boxes. Plaster
dogs they won at fairgrounds, pieces of
sea-scoured glass, the steering wheel of a
long-abandoned pedal car.
Talismans against the unknown forces of a wide
world. Certainties. Treasures.
And when they're grown they'll maybe come
across a stone their mother or father planted by
the pond – and pick it up and hold it in their
hands – and find the old lost magic once again.
A day of sun. A rock pool on a sea-loud shore.
A living moment quite untouched by time.

PETER GRAY

Dear Tom,

Do you remember how you were convinced that every tunnel we drove through on our journeys to and from school housed a dragon? Bristol is full of tunnels. The bigger the tunnel, the bigger the dragon. It stands to reason. We would toot the horn to alert the dragon we were coming, debating as to its exact whereabouts in the damp, gloomy darkness, and swerve wildly to avoid its breath of fire.

*Then, one day, I drove right into the bloody stone wall....
Our battered Citroën Diane was wedged by its bumper, impaling us, right in the dragon's lair. You yelled with delight at the delay, and faked terror that we would be*

burnt to cinders. I was much more alarmed about jamming up a dark, narrow tunnel in the middle of the rush-hour. Someone must have raised the alarm because a police car turned up fairly rapidly and sealed off both entrances with diversion signs. And you, gleeful at this new move in our game, actually told the officer that we had been swerving to avoid the dragon. He was not amused. He lifted his pen from his notepad and told you, sonny, to let your mother do the explaining.

HELEN BRAID,
FROM "LETTERS TO MY SEMI-DETACHED SON"

WIFE, THE ATHENIANS RULE THE GREEKS,
AND I RULE THE ATHENIANS, AND THOU
ME, AND OUR SON THEE; LET HIM THEN
USE SPARINGLY THE AUTHORITY WHICH
MAKES HIM, FOOLISH AS HE IS, THE MOST
POWERFUL PERSON IN GREECE.

THEMISTOCLES (C.523-C.458 B.C.)

A PROUD PARENT boasts a little of a son's abilities and his achievements. But glories in his kindness, his gentleness, his quiet courage.

PAM BROWN, b.1928

"Which one?"

DWIGHT D. EISENHOWER'S MOTHER, ON BEING ASKED IF SHE WAS PROUD OF HER SON

Nothing can come from your workshop, however rough and unfinished, that will not give me more pleasure than the most accurate thing anyone else can write.

SIR THOMAS MORE (1478-1535), TO HIS SON

A mother is proud of a son who works hard,
passes his examinations, does well in his job,
is capable and kind.
But proudest of all when she sees him in a
happy marriage, laughing with his little
child, sitting by its bed in sickness, telling it
good night tales, teaching it
a skill
... loving and beloved.

HELEN THOMSON, b.1943

If I have a monument in this world, it is my son. He is a joy, a sheer delight.

MAYA ANGELOU, b.1928

My lovely living boy,
My hope, my hap,
my love, my life,
my joy.

GUILLAUME DE SALLUSTE, SEIGNEUR
DU BARTAS, FROM *"FOURTH DAY"*

Thank you for filling a place in my life that no one else could.

PAM BROWN, b.1928

One night, I had just given Charlie a bath and as I was drying him, and powdering him and putting on his fresh nightclothes, I said all the stupid things in the world you could possibly say – things like "What a cutesy sweetsy babykins you are. You're my perfect little baby. You're my perfect goodness. Oh, I just love you and love and love you," and went on and on in that way. At some point, I looked at Charlie's face and I felt embarrassed. He looked like the wisest and most tolerant man on the Supreme Court, and I felt like a perfect fool. But then there was that other thing of Charlie's – his little twinkle. So of course, I hugged him and kissed him. There simply was great pleasure in living with Charlie, in being with him. He was so utterly civilized.

CAROL MATTHAU,
FROM *"AMONG THE PORCUPINES"*

And the exhilaration – I could have climbed Mount Everest. No post-partum depression for me! Never, never have I felt as I did then. The first time I held that baby was overwhelming. This entire complex being, twenty inches long – I examined every fingernail, tried to count his eyelashes – the smell of him – the feel. I was twenty-four and an only child, but I took to feeding and handling Steve as though I'd spent my life doing it. Whoever first said it was right – clichés are clichés because they are true. It was instinct.
I was a natural-born mother (with my own child).

LAUREN BACALL, b.1924

[Sons] have us around
their little fingers

from the moment
we set eyes on them.

ANON

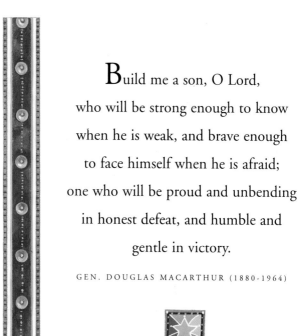

Build me a son, O Lord,
who will be strong enough to know
when he is weak, and brave enough
to face himself when he is afraid;
one who will be proud and unbending
in honest defeat, and humble and
gentle in victory.

GEN. DOUGLAS MACARTHUR (1880-1964)

Ah! happy years! once more who would not be a boy?

LORD BYRON (1788-1824), FROM *"CHILDE HAROLD'S PILGRIMAGE"*

Forgotten mornings when he walked
with his mother
Through the parables
Of sunlight
And the legend of the green chapels.

DYLAN THOMAS (1914-1953), FROM *"POEM IN OCTOBER"*

STRAINS AND PAINS AND HASSLES

He makes fuzz come out of my bald patch!

CHARLES A. LINDBERGH (1902-1974),
ABOUT HIS SON'S DRIVING

Heredity is what a man believes in until his son
begins to behave like a delinquent.

PRESBYTERIAN LIFE

A pedestrian is a man whose son
is home from college.

ANON

Poets have said the reason to have children is to give yourself immortality; and I must admit I did ask God to give me a son because I wanted someone to carry on the family name. Well, God did just that and I now confess that there have been times when I've told my son not to reveal who he is.

"You make up a name," I've said. "Just don't tell anybody who you are."

BILL COSBY, b.1937,
FROM "FATHERHOOD"

A MAN NEEDS A SON to scrunch through pebbles at his side and challenge him to skimming stones along the waves. To walk through woods and stand and listen for the stirrings in the silences. To dig and plant beside him – and pick the new potatoes from the soil. To explore the innards of an engine.

To stand and stare at excavations in the road. To run with in the summer rain. To build the winter bonfires. To work out in The Shed on spring evenings, in quiet companionship. To name the stars that prickle a frosty sky. To know he's there just as long as he's needed.

PETER GRAY

<u>GROWING PAINS...</u>

A boy becomes an adult three years before
his parents think he does, and about two
years after he thinks he does.

LEWIS B. HERSHEY

Sons turn up at posh parties with green
knees, sons put their feet through cold
frames, sons lose their brand-new sports

kits, sons scratch the car, sons have jerboas that get loose, sons forget to give you notes from school. Sons are grubby, noisy, moody and untidy – and always late.

They keep this up till their parents are plotting deportation or murder over their evening cocoa – and then, suddenly, they give themselves a shake, everything falls neatly into place – and they stand revealed as reasonable and personable young men.

PAM BROWN, b.1928

Sons fling themselves. They bounce, bump, duck, dive, slide, pound, paddle, fidget – and fall. Then they pick themselves up and do it all again.

PAM BROWN, b.1928

Having a family is like having a bowling alley installed in your brain.

MARTIN MULL

Of all the animals, the boy is the most unmanageable.

PLATO (C.428-C.348 B.C.)

How did Bill and I see our children? Were they a safety net for our marriage? When either of us stopped talking to each other... did we go to them? Did we use them for personal triumphs instead of one another? Did we involve ourselves in their lives to keep from living our own?

I broke the silence.

"Bill, how do you see our children?"

"Rarely," he grunted.

"I see them as kites," I said. "You spend a lifetime trying to get them off the ground. You run with them until you're both breathless... they crash... you add a longer tail... they hit the rooftop... you pluck them out of the spouting... you patch and comfort, adjust and teach. You watch them lifted by the wind and assure them that someday they'll fly."

Bill flipped on the light and stared at me in disbelief. "Finally, they are airborne," I continued, "but they need more string and you keep letting out and with each twist of the ball of twine, there is a sadness that goes with the joy because the kite becomes more distant and somehow you know that it won't be long until that beautiful creature will snap the lifeline that bound you together and soar as it was meant to soar... free and alone."

"Are you finished?" he finally said.

"Yes."

"Because one of your kites just hit the center garage post and he only has $100 deductible!"

ERMA BOMBECK, b.1927,
FROM *"A MARRIAGE MADE IN HEAVEN
OR TOO TIRED FOR AN AFFAIR"*

Long before a mother ceases to take care of her son he has surreptitiously started to take care of her.

PAM BROWN, b.1928

The boy was the very staff of my age, my very prop.

WILLIAM SHAKESPEARE (1564-1616),
FROM *THE MERCHANT OF VENICE*
[ACT II, SC.2, L.70]

Yᴏᴜ ᴀʀᴇ ᴀ ʜᴜᴍᴀɴ ʙᴏʏ, my young friend.

A human boy.

O glorious to be a human boy!...

O running stream of sparkling joy

To be a soaring human boy!

ᴄʜᴀʀʟᴇs ᴅɪᴄᴋᴇɴs (1812-1870),
ғʀᴏᴍ *"ʙʟᴇᴀᴋ ʜᴏᴜsᴇ"*

A boy's will is the wind's will.

And the thoughts of youth are long, long

thoughts.

ʜᴇɴʀʏ ᴡᴀᴅsᴡᴏʀᴛʜ ʟᴏɴɢғᴇʟʟᴏᴡ
(1807-1882), ғʀᴏᴍ *"ᴍʏ ʟᴏsᴛ ʏᴏᴜᴛʜ"*

He may be president, but he still comes home and swipes my socks.

JOSEPH P. KENNEDY (1888-1969)

A middle-aged son who goes up into the attic to find a half-remembered dartboard is gone for the rest of the afternoon.
He emerges filthy, happy and bearing a moth-eaten teddy, a diabolo, a bagatelle board, five jigsaws, a tin gun, fourteen scrapbooks, a box of Lego and a plastic Roman helmet.

PAM BROWN, b.1928

Sons are resigned to their mothers straightening their ties, checking their larders, dosing their colds – at fifty.

CHARLOTTE GRAY

You may be sensible and dignified and well respected – but I know that there are jellybeans in your briefcase and Bear on the wardrobe shelf.

PETER GRAY

Sons never seem to listen... and one sighs
and dismisses one's advice as so much
wasted breath.
Only to be caught up short one day by a
statement that has an oddly familiar ring.
He is quoting an impeccable source to
back his argument.
And he has forgotten it was you.

PAM BROWN, b.1928

In her heart, there's but one song: "He is coming home again." Ah! the years have been so long, now an end to hidden pain, anxious thoughts and sudden tears – son away for five long years. Such a thrill to visualize how he'll look, this precious son. Will she see, in his dear eyes, the old-time, happy glint of fun? Years have doubtless left some trace on that loved and longed-for face.

... there's but one thought: "He has journeyed one day nearer." All her dreams with prayers are fraught for his safety – no son dearer. Every morning, on her lips: "God protect all homebound ships."

WILHELMINA STITCH,
FROM *"THROUGH SUNNY WINDOWS"*

... whatever sense of hurt or injustice a man may harbour, he knows, in the depths of his soul, that his mother is waiting always for his return.

DAME ENID LYONS

One of the ironies of being a parent is that you have your children a limited number of years, and you seldom see them. You may seldom hear from them. But the power a child has over you lasts a lifetime.

BETTE DAVIS (1908-1989), FROM *"THIS 'N THAT"*

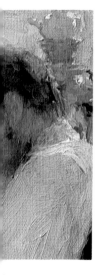

The best thing in a parent's life is to see him, long after he has grown and gone, surrounded by the things he loves, skilled, useful, happy – and yet the lad they've always known.

PAM BROWN, b.1928

Acknowledgements: The publishers are grateful for permission to reproduce copyright material. Whilst every effort has been made to trace copyright holders, the publishers would be pleased to hear from any not here acknowledged. LAUREN BACALL: Extract from *By Myself* reprinted by permission of Random House, UK. ALAN BECK: Extracts from *What is a Boy?* A pamphlet distributed by New England Insurance Co Boston, 1956. ERMA BOMBECK: Extract from *A Marriage Made in Heaven or Too Tired for an Affair.* © Erma Bombeck 1993. Reprinted by permission of Robson Books Ltd and HarperCollins*Publishers*, USA. HELEN BRAID: Extract from *Letters to My Semi-Detached Son*, first published by The Women's Press Ltd, 1993, 34 Great Sutton Street, London EC1V 0DX, reprinted on pages 24/25 is used by permission of The Women's Press Ltd. CAROL MATTHAU: Extract from *Among the Porcupines.* © Carol Matthau 1992. Reprinted by permission of Orion Publishing Group. WILHELMINA STITCH: Extract from "The Son Returns", from *Through Sunny Windows,* reprinted by permission of Sheil Land Associates Ltd. DYLAN THOMAS: Extract from "Poem in October", from *Collected Poems of Dylan Thomas.* Reprinted by permission of David Higham Associates Ltd.

Picture Credits: Exley Publications is very grateful to the following individuals and organizations for permission to reproduce their pictures: Alinari (ALI), Archiv für Kunst (AKG), Art Resource (AR), Bulloz (BU), The Bridgeman Art Library (BAL), Edimedia (EDM), Giraudon (GIR), Sotheby's Transparency Library (STL):